SAFE AND SOUND?

A guide to church security

SAFE AND SOUND?
A guide to church security

by Geoff Crago
and Graham Jeffery

Church House Publishing
Church House, Great Smith Street, London SW1P 3NZ

The Council for the Care of Churches
acknowledges with grateful thanks sponsorship of this
book by the Ecclesiastical Insurance Group.

ISBN 0 7151 7569 6

Published 1996 by Church House Publishing for the Council for
the Care of Churches, Fielden House, Little College Street,
London SW1P 3SH

Design by Krystyna Hewitt
Printed in Great Britain by
Stephens and George Ltd

Dear Lord,
You became nothing
So we could have everything.
Help us to keep what is entrusted to us with care,
That what is bestowed upon us,
May be shared freely with others.
Amen.

THE ONLY CHURCH THAT MATTERS

Your church is unique – no two are exactly the same. So the ways in which you use it and look after it are unique as well.

There is no blueprint for church security which will be right for every single church. But there are a number of common sense things that you can do to protect your church and its contents. That's what this book is about.

The first thing is to take a careful look at your church and its place in the community.

What are the factors that make your church unique? For example:

- *its setting* – rural, suburban, city centre
- *its surroundings* – open country, houses, commercial property
- *its character* – plain and functional, contemporary, medieval tourist 'gem'
- *its role* – open and used daily, weekly or infrequently
- *its availability* – locked or unlocked, manned or unmanned

Only you can make an assessment of these things – because it is your church. The answers you come up with will affect the way you think about security matters. What would be ideal for a small country church would be totally inappropriate for a great town church or a church/hall on a major housing estate.

It pays to involve a wide cross-section of people in the discussion of these questions – because security isn't just the responsibility of the clergy and church officers.

Everyone in the church community should be involved – and friends of the church who may not be regular members of the congregation.

Assess the situation together; identify the particular needs of your church and community; and then draw up a security policy. It is useful to appoint one person as co-ordinator to make sure the policy is carried out, progress monitored and changes implemented when necessary.

If people are consulted about these matters, there is a much better chance of them playing their part in church security and seeing it as the responsibility of the whole community.

If a church is left open during the day, it is a good idea to have a rota of people on duty to welcome visitors and keep an eye on the church and its contents. Not only is this common sense from a security point of view, but it provides a human face and a point of contact. Many churches see this as a vital aspect of ministry – and lay people are happy to be involved.

It may not always be possible to have someone on duty in the church whenever it is unlocked. But entry should be by one door only and the rest locked – subject, of course, to sensible provision for escape in the event of fire.

Consider establishing the ecclesiastical equivalent of 'Neighbourhood Watch'. This has been done in a number of areas and called 'Church Watch'. Quite often several churches in a locality get together – often under the auspices of a council of churches, a 'Churches Together' group or some other natural geographical grouping.

Any 'Church Watch' scheme should be set up in consultation with the Crime Prevention Officer of your local police and the co–ordinator of Neighbourhood Watch. Even if no formal 'Church Watch' is set up, it's a good idea to talk to the co–ordinator of Neighbourhood Watch about the particular problems of protecting your church. (See appendix for details of a free booklet: *Setting up and running a local church watch*)

There are also steps you can take on an informal basis. If people live close to the church, ask them specifically to keep an eye on it and report anything suspicious. If your church is in a town or city centre, you could, perhaps, ask local shopkeepers or office staff to do the same.

Why not suggest that parishioners call in to the church as often as they can when walking the dog, doing the shopping or driving past in the car?

Your church really is unique and it is there for the community to use and visit. If members of the local community – church-goers or not – feel that they have an interest in 'their' church, then they will be happy to play their part, however small, in keeping an eye on it, protecting it and preserving it for themselves and for future generations.

A church which is seen to be regularly used
and visited, which is clean, tidy and well
maintained is far less likely to become the
target of thieves and vandals.

WHAT HAVE WE HERE?

If your church was the target of thieves or vandals would you know precisely what was taken or damaged?

Would you have clear descriptions of stolen items?

Would you immediately be able to give the police the sort of information they would need to recover and identify stolen items?

Would you be able to give the same information to your insurers – together with an accurate valuation?

In the event of vandalism or fire, would you have photographs or drawings to help with the repair or replacement of damaged items?

The experience of the police and insurers is that, in many instances, the answer to those questions is 'no'.

It is vital to keep up-to-date records of everything in your church and of the fabric, fixtures and fittings of the building.

An inventory is essential and should contain details of everything – even those items to which you never even give a second thought. You may think that a piece of furniture, a key, a set of organ pipes or a hundred and one other items have little or no value and no-one would ever steal them. But your knowledge of the 'market' may not be as good as the thief's.

The Council for the Care of Churches publishes a *Church Property Register* which indicates exactly what needs to be recorded. Include everything – with accurate descriptions and measurements. Note markings and hallmarks, scratches, dents and imperfections. Careful recording of these details can turn a common item into something unique and easily identifiable.

In addition to the written inventory, you should photograph each item. Use a competent photographer and photograph one object at a time with as much detail as possible. Remember to show a ruler in the background to help with identifying size. Prints are better than slides – you can keep the negatives and use them to make enlargements should any item be stolen or destroyed. The prints and negatives should be carefully labelled so that they can be matched to the description in the inventory.

SMILE Please

As well as the more obvious valuables (communion plate, silverware, etc.) the records should include items of furniture (fixed or movable), musical instruments, paintings and pictures (and frames), textiles (altar frontals, vestments, wall hangings), statues and carvings, carpets, doors, door fittings (locks, handles and hinges), memorials, architectural features and stained glass.

It is also a good idea to make a comprehensive video record of your church – its architecture, windows, features and contents. The inventory, photographs and video should then be stored in a safe place – away from the church – and kept up to date.

Valuation is one of the most difficult aspects of the recording process. But for reasons of insurance as well as security it is important to include accurate and realistic valuations of the contents of your church. Although it is not necessary to insure for full replacement value (see *A Policy for Insurance* below), good valuations are needed. If in doubt, consult a recognised expert.

Finally, check the contents of your church against the inventory at regular intervals. It is not unknown for an item to be stolen and nobody notice for days, weeks or even months.

If items are stolen, the existence of a good inventory makes recovery much more likely.

THE VIEW
FROM
OUTSIDE

What does your church look like to the prospective thief or vandal?

It would, in theory, be possible to make your church look like a high-security prison – with high fences, closed-circuit television, guard dogs and alarms. No one would get in – but would you want your church to look like a fortress?

At the other extreme, some churches are an open invitation to the thief, vandal or arsonist.

So take a walk around the church and look with the eyes of a prospective thief or vandal. Then – as a first line of defence – think about these common-sense precautions:

Keep boundary walls and fences in good repair. Improve all-round visibility by trimming hedges and trees. But keep boundary hedges thick and difficult to penetrate. Hawthorn, hedging rose and holly provide a good, natural deterrent.

Keep points of access to a sensible minimum. Perhaps you should lock all the gates at night.

Restrict vehicle access by locking double gates. (Removing large objects is much easier if the thief can drive right up to the door.)

Bright lighting is a good deterrent. Use PIR (Passive Infra Red) devices around the exterior. These switch on bright lights automatically at night when someone passes the sensor.

Where appropriate, place PIR controlled lights on the roof to deter lead and copper thieves. These metals are popular with thieves and easy to dispose of. Not only are they expensive to replace, but the loss may not even be noticed until the next heavy downpour. It could then be too late to prevent severe water damage to the church interior.

Make sure that the boiler house,
oil or gas store, and churchyard
equipment store are all secure.
Mowers and other equipment
should be clearly marked with the
name and postcode of the church.
Ladders should be kept secure and
out of sight.

If there are drainpipes, consider the use of
anti-climb paint.

A pile of bricks or stones is a source of
ammunition for a vandal – or an aid to entry
for the thief. Remove them.

Consider exterior anti-vandal protection for stained glass windows.

Consult your insurers and the Crime Prevention Officer of your local police about any additional precautions which may be appropriate for your church.

GETTING IN

Take another walk around the church building –
again looking with the eyes of a thief or vandal –
and count up how many possible points of entry
there are. Many churches have several doors as
well as windows, trap doors to cellar or boiler
house, roof and tower access points. Are they all
really secure?

It is important that good quality locks, bolts and hinges are used on all doors and other access points. It is no use having high security locks on one door and a simple domestic lock on another. Similarly the value of a high security lock will be wasted if the door itself is not suitably strong or the door frame is inadequately installed.

Opening window lights should be fitted with approved locks and, where appropriate, consideration should be given to bars or grills. But seek advice from your architect and church authorities first.

The aim is to make access simple for those who have a right to get in, whilst making it difficult for the thief or vandal.

Some people, cleaners, flower arrangers, organists etc., need a key, but not necessarily one each. The number of keys in circulation should be limited and carefully controlled.

A record should be kept of all keys and key holders. The practice of 'getting an extra one cut' is to be discouraged. You need to know exactly who has access to the church. The establishment of simple systems and procedures for the issuing of keys is essential for security. Ideally, only one door should be the recognised access point and all others normally kept locked. This will hinder the opportunist thief.

Keys should never be hidden 'in a safe place' in the church or porch. Thieves know where to look. And keys should never be left in the lock.

Each church should have a 'secure area' which can be kept locked even when the building is open to the public. The vestry may be the obvious place for this – but, in reality, vestries are often among the least secure areas of the church.

Consider the creation of a secure area if one does not exist, or upgrade the vestry with window bars, high security locks etc.

Some churches – though not by any means all – would benefit from the installation of alarm systems and closed-circuit television. This depends on the individual circumstances, but do not install any system before seeking the advice and approval of your insurers.

"Ours was open at Exodus Chapter 22."

STOP THIEF

Almost anything can have a value to thieves –
and they will sometimes come with a
shopping list.

Never think 'No-one could possibly want to
steal that!'. The chances are that
somewhere, something very like it has
already been stolen.

It isn't only the more obvious valuables that need protection. Of course we always lock up the silver in the safe. But what about that little Jacobean table? Easy to pick up and take away in the boot of an ordinary car. Before anyone notices, it's a hundred miles away and being sold in an antique shop.

Items like that can never be 100% secure – but you can make life more difficult for the thief – perhaps by a secure chain and bolt attached to the wall or floor.

Again, it is common sense – thinking
the way a thief might think, and trying
to be one step ahead.

Madonna Protecting her Child. XIV century.

You need to go round your church and look carefully at all the contents, fixtures and fittings – and architectural features – and work out the best way of protecting them.

Church plate – keep in the safe when not in use. But is the safe really safe? Many church safes are totally inadequate. Some are easy to lift and remove. Some have such thin backs that a tin–opener would open them up. Consider fixing the safe to the floor or bricking it into a wall. If in doubt, seek advice.

Never leave the safe key on the premises.

Cross and candlesticks – can be very
attractive to thieves. Consider substituting with
replicas of base metal or wood during the week
and keeping the best set in the safe or a secure
area. It may also be necessary to remove other
portable items to a secure area when the church
is not in use.

Exceptionally valuable items are often safer if
removed to a bank vault or lodged in a
cathedral treasury or
local museum on
indefinite loan.

Now look at some other items which will need protection:

- Furniture (including large items like pews, chests, cupboards).
- Lecterns, fonts and altar tables (often very 'collectable').
- Statues and carvings.
- Glassware.
- Stained glass windows (whole windows are sometimes stolen).
- Electronic items – microphones, amplifiers, computer equipment, tape decks etc.

All valuable items should be 'identity marked' with
the name of the church and the postcode. Different
materials require different methods of marking.
Special care is needed when marking historic items
– seek advice first.

If theft occurs, always report it to the police and
your insurers – and do so quickly. Any delay could
mean the difference between recovering an item
and losing it for ever.

Some thefts from churches are purely opportunist: but more and more are professionally planned and executed. Never think: 'It couldn't happen in our church'. It could – and, unless you take these common sense precautions, it probably will.

SECURE FROM FIRE

The results of fire – either accidental or deliberate –
can be disastrous. Arson is a particular risk for
churches and must be regarded as a security
problem. You need to protect your church and its
contents as effectively as possible.

Specific advice about fire prevention can be
obtained from the Fire Prevention Officer of your
local fire brigade and from your insurers.

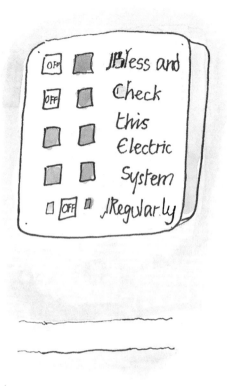

Electrical systems, heating equipment and lightning conductors should all be regularly inspected and serviced by professionals. The church should be equipped with appropriate fire extinguishers and these, too, should be regularly inspected and serviced. Make sure that everyone using the building knows where the extinguishers are and how to use them.

Take great care when using electrical appliances or portable heaters. Ensure that equipment is turned off when not in use and electricity disconnected.

Fires caused by lack of maintenance or carelessness are one thing – arson is, in many ways, a far more serious threat.

Experience shows that many church fires are started by thieves – both adults and children. If anyone is determined to start a fire they will probably succeed. But don't make it easy for them.

Many churches have all the necessary material to hand for the arsonist:

- The box of matches by the altar for lighting candles

- The pile of old newspapers or service sheets

- New or part–used candles

- The can of petrol for the mower

You might as well put up a notice saying *'Fire-lighting materials – help yourself'*.

In event of FIRE, please phone NOAH 0127

WATER

So, once again, common sense and vigilance are needed. Keep matches, candles and other ignition sources locked away. Do not allow piles of combustible rubbish to accumulate. Make sure that petrol, central heating oil, gas cylinders and other fuels are stored securely.

Smoking should be strictly forbidden.

Always lock the church at night.

There let it for thy glory burn, an inextinguishable blaze

A POLICY FOR INSURANCE

Adequate insurance for your church is an absolute 'must'.

Church insurance is a specialist market. Those companies which do specialise in it have the expertise to advise you and arrange the appropriate cover for your particular church.

In all matters concerning church security you need to be aware of the insurance implications.

Insurance cover should be reviewed
regularly with your insurers in order to
keep the policy up-to-date. Valuations
may need to be revised; items of
property may need to be added or
removed; or new building work might
affect the insurance requirements. Just
like any insurance policy, your church
insurance must be adequate to meet your
current needs. This is another reason for
knowing exactly what you have in your
church and keeping an up-to-date
inventory.

Policies vary greatly from company to company. You should be aware of exactly what is – and is not – covered by your policy, and whether there are any special terms and conditions.

Some policies specify a 'single article limit' above which they will not pay out on a particular item. If there are items of particular value, specific cover can be arranged for them.

Many valuable, named items are often not insured for their full 'saleroom value' (their value as an antique in the secular market) because they are unique, could probably not be sold anyway, and could not possibly be replaced. To insure at full 'saleroom value' might mean prohibitive premiums and special security conditions being imposed by insurers. An example of this is a fine Elizabethan chalice – valued by a London saleroom at £10,000 which may, in fact, be insured for only £2000 – the cost of a 'worthy modern replacement'.

It is essential to understand the cover provided by your policy. If in doubt, consult your insurers. They will advise you and make sure that the policy is appropriate and adequate.

You should keep your policy documents and contact telephone numbers and addresses with the inventory in a safe place away from the church building. They will be no use to you if they are destroyed in a fire at the church or stolen with the safe.

HELP!

A great deal of help and assistance is available to you from:

The Crime Prevention Officer of your local police

The Fire Prevention Officer of your local fire brigade

Church authorities – Diocesan Advisory Committees and equivalent bodies in other denominations

The Council for the Care of Churches
Fielden House, Little College Street,
London SWlP 3SH
Tel: 0171 222 3793 Fax: 0171 222 3794

English Heritage
23 Savile Row, London W1X 1AB
Tel: 0171 973 3000 Fax: 0171 973 3001

Ecclesiastical Insurance Group
Church Insurances Department
Beaufort House, Brunswick Road,
Gloucester GL1 1JZ
Tel: 01452 528533 Fax: 01452 423557

The Fire Protection Association
Melrose Avenue, Borehamwood, Herts WD6 2BJ
Tel: 0181 207 2345 Fax: 0181 207 6305

BOOKLETS, LEAFLETS AND VIDEOS

Available from Ecclesiastical Insurance Group (address as above):
Technical Advice Sheets about Church Security, Fire Precautions and related topics

The leaflet *Setting Up and Running a Local Church Watch*

The video *Arson Alert*

Available from the Council for the Care of Churches (address as above):
The video *Looking After Your Church*

A series of booklets on various aspects of church care

Dear Lord,
No one can steal your spirit.
That is given to us daily,
   freely.

Hour by hour you love us,
   care for us,
   feed us,
   wish us well.

May we, who visit your house,
praise you and bless you.
And go out to serve you
 strengthened by your love.

Through Jesus Christ our Saviour.

St Paul's. WIGAN

VICAR · The Rev J. Cotton
Churchwarden Helen Hunt
Crime Prevention
Officer P.C. Egbert

Amen